THE VITAMIN C REVOLUTION

There is increasing awareness that vitamin C has a wide variety of roles in human health. New therapeutic uses are being actively investigated. Now a new method of preparing this vitamin has added to its effectiveness and "tamed" it for those who have reacted unfavorably to its acidity. Learn how this new form of vitamin C—enhanced by the power of its C metabolites—is revolutionizing the way clinicians and nutritionists think about health and disease.

ABOUT THE AUTHOR

Jeffrey Bland, PhD is CEO of HealthComm International, Inc., a leading global health communications firm, located in Gig Harbor, Washington. Before founding HealthComm, Dr. Bland was for 13 years a professor of chemistry at the University of Puget Sound in Tacoma, Washington. He is a former Senior Research Scientist at the Linus Pauling Institute of Science and Medicine and former director of a large medical laboratory in Washington State. Dr. Bland lectures widely on health and nutrition and has written and edited numerous books and articles for the scientific and popular press, including several works in the Good Health Guide series and the second of Keats Publishing's annual survey series, *A Year in Nutritional Medicine.*

VITAMIN C: THE FUTURE IS NOW

C METABOLITES, THREONATE, AND THE POWER OF ESTER-C®

Jeffrey Bland, Ph.D.
author of *Nutraerobics*

Keats Publishing, Inc., New Canaan, Connecticut

Good Health Guides are published by
Keats Publishing, Inc.
27 Pine Street, P.O. Box 876
New Canaan, Connecticut 06840

CONTENTS

INTRODUCTION

FROM CURING SCURVY TO PREVENTING DEGENERATIVE DISEASES

Vitamin C (ascorbic acid) has been a nutrient of great interest and controversy for the nutritional supplement-taking public for more than 30 years, and for good reason. Scientific studies have indicated that the role of vitamin C in preserving health extends far beyond the prevention of the vitamin deficiency disease called scurvy. Medical and nutritional research now suggests that vitamin C is potentially important for the prevention of certain forms of cancer, heart disease and some forms of allergic disorders, the maintenance of fertility in males, the prevention and possible treatment of viral infections including the common cold and flu, and for the support of proper immune function.[1-6]

Recently James Enstrom, PhD published a paper in which he suggested that individuals who regularly supplement their diet with vitamin C have a statistically significant increase in life expectancy over those who consume lower amounts of vitamin C.[7] Although this study does not prove that vitamin C is the sole factor responsible for prolonging the lives of those who take it, it does suggest that vitamin C may be very important in reducing the risk of a number of age-related diseases which compromise our health.

Many people regularly supplement their diet with vitamin C. In the United States, this prevalence can vary from as low as 10 percent of the population as a whole to more than 40 percent for older individuals.[8,9] People who are interested in supplementing with vitamin C would like to know certain things about this nutrient, including answers to the following questions:

How much should I take?
What type of vitamin C is the best?
Are there any problems in taking too much vitamin C?

Over the past few years, scientists have begun to find the answers to these questions. In this Good Health Guide we will explore the present state of understanding of these questions. Tremendous advances have recently been made in understanding the physiological effects and human biochemistry of vitamin C, at both traditional nutritional levels of intake (at or about equal to the Recommended Dietary Allowance level) and at higher doses.[10] What this research indicates is that vitamin C is one of the safest nutrients in our diet, with a range of safety in excess of 100 times the RDA. The research also indicates that the role of vitamin C in human physiology is much more complex than was previously thought, and that it plays a role in numerous metabolic functions.

The isolation of vitamin C from various foods occurred nearly 70 years ago. This major medical advance made it possible to prevent scurvy, a disease that had killed vast numbers of people throughout history. For much of the past 70 years the research on vitamin C focused on understanding and preventing this dreaded disease. During the past decade, however, there has been an explosion of new information about the other health benefits of vitamin C, focusing on its role in improving physiological function and preventing various diseases. We now recognize that establishing the RDA level for vitamin C—the amount needed to prevent vitamin C deficiency and scurvy—defined only part of the benefit. We also need to know the amount of vitamin C which is optimal to promote health and reduce the risk of other diseases that may be related to the suboptimal intake of the vitamin C.[11]

The recognition that the benefits of vitamin C extend beyond the prevention and treatment of diseases like scurvy arose from the pioneering work of Irwin Stone, PhD, Frederick Klenner, MD, Emanuel Cheraskin, MD, DMD, and two-time Nobel Prize Laureate Linus Pauling, PhD.[12-15] Their pioneering work opened the door for such modern vitamin C investigators as Mark Levine, MD, PhD from the National Institutes of Health, Anthony Verlangieri, PhD from the University of Mississippi, and Balz Frei, PhD from Harvard University Medical School.[16-18] Their work has now determined that vitamin C intake above the present RDA is necessary to meet the physiological needs of the "well" person and may be considerably higher still in the sick individual.[19]

The health benefits of vitamin C derive from a variety of interrelated substances called vitamin C metabolites,[20] such as dehydroascorbate and threonate. Recently, a new form of vitamin C has been developed which contains both ascorbic acid in the neutralized ascorbate form as well as vitamin C metabolites. This new form of vitamin C, called Ester-C®, is produced in a buffered form with minerals such as calcium, potassium, sodium, magnesium or zinc. It is better tolerated by people whose digestive systems are sensitive to ordinary ascorbic acid.

Ester-C as a buffered form of vitamin C also contains the natural vitamin C metabolites dehydroascorbate (DHA) and threonate, which will be discussed in this booklet. These metabolites have beneficial influence on the cellular utilization of vitamin C and potentially on other nutrients as well.

HOW MUCH IS ENOUGH?

With a number of essential processes dependent upon adequate levels of vitamin C, scientists have heatedly debated the RDAs for vitamin C. The RDA for any nutrient is defined as "the level of intake necessary to meet the needs of practically all healthy people." For vitamin C, therefore, the RDA is the amount required to prevent scurvy, with the addition of a safety factor to account for differences in people. This definition does not take into account the presence in the body of literally hundreds of different enzymes which require vitamin C to work correctly, or the optimal amount of vitamin C which would serve as an effective antioxidant.

During the past few years, Mark Levine, MD, PhD of the National Institutes of Health has been performing the most exacting studies ever undertaken to determine the amount of vitamin C necessary to promote proper metabolic function. Based upon his sophisticated enzyme analysis method, Dr. Levine has concluded that the RDA for vitamin C is too low and should be several times higher than the present level.[21]

The minimum amount of vitamin C required to prevent scurvy (the disease which represents the last stage of vitamin C deficiency) is reasonably easy to ascertain. In numerous studies over the past four decades, scientists have determined that 10 milligrams of vitamin C per day will prevent scurvy in most people. In establishing a daily intake of vitamin C that would prevent scurvy and allow for adequate reserves of ascorbic acid, the Food and Nutrition Board of the National Research Council in 1989 recommended a daily intake (RDA) of 60 milligrams for the average healthy adult. This level of vitamin C intake and the others listed below create body pools of ascorbic acid large enough to protect against scurvy for 30 to 45 days if vitamin C ingestion is suddenly stopped.

The National Research Council did recognize that smoking causes the body to use vitamin C more quickly and suggested that for smokers the vitamin C intake should be 100 mg a day. This was the first time the RDAs had taken into account the importance of environment and lifestyle factors in establishing the need for a vitamin, and it reflects a change in thinking by the scientific community, which had previously regarded a single amount as being adequate for everyone.

Table 1

U.S. Recommended Dietary Allowances (RDA) for vitamin C

Individual	Age	RDA (mg/day)
Infants	to 6 mo.	30
	6 mo.-1 yr.	35
Children	1-3	40
	4-10	45
Adolescents	11-14	50
Adults	15+	60
Pregnant women		70
Lactating women		95
Smokers		100

Source: Recommended Dietary Allowances, 10th edition.[22]

Although a daily intake of 60 mg of vitamin C may be enough to prevent scurvy in normal adults, it may not be enough to satisfy all the body's needs for ascorbic acid. The level of vitamin C necessary for optimal health is difficult to estimate. Biochemical analyses, comparison of amounts required by other animals, analysis of primitive diets, and evolutionary history have all helped to determine the ideal consumption of vitamin C.

This debate would be pointless if we knew exactly how much vitamin C was required to fulfill the specific needs of each ascorbate-dependent body process. It is surprising—considering the very long historical interest in vitamin C—that so little information exists at the present time to guide us. A few biochemical requirements are understood in fine detail. For example, the highest concentration of vitamin C in the body is found in the adrenal glands. Dr. Mark Levine has found that the production of the adrenal hormone norepinephrine is very sensitive to the availability of vitamin C. He and his colleagues are performing experiments to determine what level of vitamin C best supports norepinephrine production. When this work is complete, we face a similar task with the hundreds of other functions.

Often, when scientific studies cannot be done conveniently with humans, researchers turn to animal models for answers. In the case of vitamin C, choosing an animal alternative is not a simple decision. After vitamin C had been identified several decades ago, researchers discovered an astonishing fact: Most animals synthesize their own vitamin C and do not need it in their diet. Whether or not they manufacture enough vitamin C to promote optimum health, considering environmental stress, energy expenditure and other factors, is currently being studied. The human, other primates, the guinea pig, the red-vented bulbul (a fruit- and berry-eating Asian bird), the Indian fruit-eating bat, the rainbow trout and the Coho salmon are the only animals on Earth which do not produce their own vitamin C.

These animals, including humans, went against 425 million years of evolution during which the rest of the animals produced ascorbic acid internally. These innovators discarded the cumbersome metabolic machinery that turns the simple sugar, glucose, into ascorbic acid, and became dependent on dietary consumption of this important nutrient.

Comparing the relative quantities of vitamin C synthesized by certain mammals with recommended human consumption levels suggests that the RDA might be disturbingly low. The level of ascorbic acid manufactured by most mammals varies considerably with their stress levels: As sickness or stress increases, mammals manufacture much more vitamin C. Unstressed goats, for example, manufacture 33 mg per kilogram of body weight per day (mg/kg/day). This amount can increase to as much as 190 mg/kg/day—a six-fold increase—when goats are stressed. For humans of average weight, the RDA for vitamin C converts to only 0.9 mg/kg/day. The following table, a compilation of data from several studies, demonstrates how much vitamin C some animals normally produce. (Where data are available, a range is given.)

Table 2

Rates of Ascorbic Acid Synthesis in Mammals

Species	Synthetic Rate (mg/kg/day)	
	Low	High
Goat	33	190
Cow	16	18
Sheep	25	
Rat	39	199
Mouse	34	275
Squirrel	29	
Gerbil	25	
Rabbit	9	226
Cat	5	40
Dog	5	40
Pig	8	
Human (RDA)	0.9	

Source: Mark Levine, "New concepts in the biology and biochemistry of ascorbic acid," *New England Journal of Medicine*, 314: 892-902 (1986).

Investigators in South Africa measured vitamin C levels in baboons captured in the wild and found that the animals required 10 mg/kg/day of vitamin C to sustain the level of vitamin C found in their blood at the time of capture. In other studies, investigators determined that vervet monkeys require only 0.5 to 0.7 mg/kg/day to prevent scurvy (similar to the RDA for humans), but need 3 to 8 mg/kg/day to maintain the plasma ascorbic acid levels recorded at their capture.

The Subcommittee on Laboratory Animal Nutrition of the National Research Council has researched the optimal levels of nutrients for most laboratory animals. Normalizing their findings to an animal of 70 kg (the average weight of adult males), the subcommittee recommends that most primates be fed 1.75 to 3.5 grams of vitamin C per day. This is very similar to the relative amount of vitamin C synthesized by the goat, rat and mouse—after adjustment for weight.

Guinea pigs need only 1.5 mg/kg/day to prevent scurvy—slightly more than the RDA for humans, but research by M.S. Yew showed that they need 16 mg/kg/day for optimal growth and health, and 50 mg/kg/day for recovery from surgery and anesthesia.[23]

These animal studies demonstrate the enormous discrepancy between the amount of vitamin C required to prevent scurvy and that required for optimal health. After considering the implications of these studies, Dr. Linus Pauling recommended that humans consume between 2.3 and 10 grams of vitamin C per day.

Another model consulted in weighing recommendations for optimal human consumption of vitamin C is that presented by investigations into primitive diets. Drs. S. Boyd Eaton and Melvin Konner have closely studied the diets of primitive tribes throughout the world. They contend these tribes presently consume diets similar to those of our remote human ancestors—diets to which humans have genetically adapted over thousands of years.[24] According to Eaton and Konner's investigations, humans are genetically programmed to thrive on a diet that includes daily levels of at least 400 mg of vitamin C. Along with a number of other substantial dietary changes introduced over the most recent 100 years of man's history on the planet, reduced vitamin C consumption might contribute to the epidemic of chronic degenerative diseases in modern humans.

BEYOND SCURVY

PHYSIOLOGY OR PHARMACOLOGY?

Many researchers and health professionals make the distinction between physiologic and pharmacologic doses of vitamin C. Any dosage near the RDA is considered physiologic, or necessary for bodily function. Any intake substantially above the RDA is labeled pharmacologic or therapeutic. The evidence presented previously from studies of animals and primitive cultures suggests that daily consumption of up to 500 mg of vitamin C may be considered physiologic.

It is especially important to distinguish between physiologic and pharmacologic intakes of vitamin C when we consider the growing evidence that large, pharmacologic doses of vitamin C—1 gram and more—can ameliorate a variety of health problems. Like the animals mentioned earlier which dramatically increase their synthesis of vitamin C when stressed, humans need and respond to large doses of vitamin C when sick.

Although he was not the first investigator to suggest it, Dr. Linus Pauling focused worldwide attention on his theory that vitamin C helps manage everything from the common cold to cancer. He originally suggested that moderate doses of vitamin C—250 to 1000 mg—can halt the spread of viral and bacterial infections, and that large doses—one gram or more—can kill those infections. Based on personal research and experience, Pauling later advocated 1–3 grams for prevention and 8–10 grams for cure.

Pauling's pronouncement was considered irresponsible and heretical by many in the medical field. But up until his death at the age of 93, Pauling vigorously advocated the pharmacologic uses of vitamin C. A growing body of evidence now supports him.

PREVENTING THE COMMON COLD

How Vitamin C Works on Symptoms

Linus Pauling based many of the conclusions in his book *Vitamin C and the Common Cold*[25] on a number of earlier studies that tested the effectiveness of vitamin C in preventing or reducing symptoms of the common cold. Probably the most striking study cited by Pauling was performed by Dr. G. Ritzel, a physician with the school medical service of the city of Basel, Switzerland.

Ritzel performed a double-blind, placebo-controlled study using 279 boys at a ski resort. The test group of children received 1000-mg. ascorbic acid tablets every morning; the control group received placebo tablets. While the investigation progressed, neither the boys nor the investigators knew which pill was the placebo and which the vitamin C. At the end of the study, an independent group analyzed the results. They found the vitamin C group had 61 percent fewer days of illness and 64 percent fewer symptoms per person than the placebo group.

Pauling's book created a stir in the medical community, as investigators scrambled to prove (or disprove) his hypothesis. As a result, a number of excellent, precise studies have confirmed the effectiveness of vitamin C in combating the common cold. The first, performed in 1972 in Toronto, Canada, involved 407 subjects receiving ascorbic acid (1 gram per day plus 3 grams per day for three days at the onset of illness); 411 subjects received a placebo. Over a four-month period, the group receiving vitamin C was house-bound 30 percent less and missed 33 percent fewer days of work than the control group.

In another study, half of 112 Canadian soldiers in the midst of operational training received 1 gram of vitamin C per day. The other half received a placebo. Over the four weeks of the study, the soldiers receiving vitamin C had 68 percent fewer sick days than the placebo group.

There have been numerous other studies with less dramatic results. Some showed no benefit of vitamin C therapy, but these studies often contained glaring bias or inappropriate methodology. The evidence from vitamin C studies overwhelmingly demonstrates that vitamin C therapy, if begun at the onset of symptoms, lessens the severity and length of cold infections. Researchers are less sure vitamin C therapy prevents colds, although some evidence suggests that it may.

FIGHTING OTHER VIRAL AND BACTERIAL INFECTIONS

How Vitamin C Works on Infections

The common cold is actually a viral infection. Colds are hard to avoid because the virus mutates and adapts rapidly to changing environments. Colds are hard to shake off because there are no prescription drugs that can safely interrupt the life cycle of this virus. Nevertheless, vitamin C relieves the symptoms and shortens the duration of colds because, in large doses, it has demonstrated antiviral characteristics. These same characteristics make vitamin C effective in the fight against a variety of other viral illnesses.

In a study of a group of individuals suffering from cold sores (actually a manifestation of the viral herpes type I infection), a daily administration of 1800 mg of a vitamin C bioflavonoid complex significantly shortened sore healing time. The placebo group healed in an average of 10 days, and the test group healed in 4.5 days.[26]

Vitamin C can also fight hepatitis infections that sometimes result from blood transfusions. In a controlled study in Japan, 1,100 patients who were given daily dosages of 2 grams of vitamin C after surgery requiring blood transfusions had absolutely no hepatitis infections. Seven percent of 150 control patients who did not receive vitamin C, however, were infected with the hepatitis virus.[27]

The antiviral properties of ascorbic acid have been known almost since the vitamin's discovery. Even before the discovery of the polio vaccine, Dr. Claus Jungeblut, working at the College of Physicians and Surgeons of Columbia University, used high doses of vitamin C to inactivate the poliomyelitis virus and arrest its paralyzing effect. He went on to use vitamin C successfully against the herpes, vaccinia, and hepatitis viruses. Interest in these clinical successes against polio evaporated after the development of the polio vaccine. But they demonstrate an antiviral capability of vitamin C that could make it effective against such modern viral maladies as Epstein-Barr and chronic fatigue syndrome.

Researchers have recently found that vitamin C is helpful in protecting against bacterial effects of *Helicobacter pylori*, which is associated with gastritis and stomach cancer.[28] Many researchers believe that continual irritation of the stomach lining produced by infection with this bacterium not only causes ulceration, but may increase susceptibility to stomach cancer. Vitamin C may prove to be an important tool to reduce the risk of these conditions.

Robert Cathcart, MD, has developed a procedure for administering vitamin C to his patients who have colds or the flu. He instructs these patients to take supplemental vitamin C up to the point where they develop diarrhea, a point he calls "bowel tolerance." From that level he has them reduce the dose slightly to stop the diarrhea. Using this technique, Dr. Cathcart has treated what he calls "10-gram-or-more flu," which means the individual took more than 10 grams of vitamin C without producing diarrhea when he or she had a cold or flu. He has noted that most people can tolerate a much higher dose of vitamin C without producing diarrhea when they are ill than when they are well, because, he believes, they need more of the nutrient when they are sick. (Dr. Cathcart's method of vitamin C administration is described in detail in the Keats Good Health Guide *Vitamin C Updated.*) In a sense, he suggests that a person can "titrate" the need for vitamin C based upon bowel tolerance of the vitamin. Although this hypothesis has not been subjected to a controlled trial, Dr. Cathcart has reported success in treating thousands of patients by this method.

BOLSTERING IMMUNITY

How Vitamin C Helps White Blood Cells Fight Disease

Vitamin C helps fight viral and bacterial infections in part because of its influence over immune function and bactericidal activity of infection-fighting cells in the body. Leukocytes, one type of white blood cells, are an extremely important part of the immune system. They contain a very high concentration of ascorbic acid that decreases with infection and returns to normal after recovery.

The relationship between vitamin C and leukocytes was accidentally discovered by researchers using guinea pigs to study leukocyte function. The researchers became increasingly frustrated because sample leukocytes they extracted from their laboratory guinea pigs were unusually fragile. Upon discovering that the animals were slightly scorbutic, they realized that vitamin C might have a profound influence on leukocyte health.

The more vitamin C is depleted from leukocytes, the more severe the cold symptoms, for example. During an infection, leukocytes actively absorb orally administered doses of vitamin C.[29] A variety of other agents also deplete leukocyte concentrations of vitamin C. Steroid therapy, birth control pills, stress and cigarette smoking, all of which are known to compromise the immune system, deplete leukocytes of ascorbic acid. Vitamin C supplementation corrects these deficits.

One type of leukocyte, the neutrophil, contains an extremely high concentration of vitamin C. Neutrophils isolated from rabbits or guinea pigs have ascorbic acid concentrations 10 to 40 times those of whole blood. Vitamin C supplementation is particularly effective in increasing the phagocytic activity, or killing response, of ascorbic acid-deficient neutrophils. It is thought that vitamin C enhances the function of many types of leukocytes by inactivating free radicals and other toxicants produced during phagocytosis of foreign material.

The production of interferon, an immune-stimulant substance secreted by lymphocytes, also seems to be enhanced by vitamin C supplementation. Mice fed an ascorbic acid-supplemented diet demonstrate increased circulating levels of interferon when given a viral challenge.[30] On the basis of this and other studies, Pauling contended that expensive interferon drug treatment in immune-compromised patients is unnecessary because inexpensive vitamin C therapy fulfills the same function.

Raxit Jariwalla, PhD, a senior scientist at the Linus Pauling Institute of Science and Medicine, recently found that vitamin C may also aid in activating response to the human immunodeficiency virus (HIV). In cell culture work, when vitamin C was added in large quantity to a medium containing HIV-infected human white blood cells, the infected cells died more quickly, leaving behind the healthy cells.[31] Vitamin C is also necessary for proper adrenal function. Adrenal response is a vital part of the battle against disease. The production of the hormone norepinephrine is dependent upon vitamin C. Norepinephrine is responsible for the "rush" of adrenaline; it fulfills the same function as direct stimulation of the parasympathetic nervous system. Other adrenal hormones, similarly dependent upon vitamin C for their production, are responsible for a variety of functions essential to normal health, including curbing the inflammatory response. For all these reasons, the human immune and endocrine systems are severely compromised without an adequate intake of vitamin C.

How Vitamin C Works on Cancer

The essential role of vitamin C in maintaining the healthy state of the immune system is one reason it helps prevent cancer. In addition, its cancer-protective effect stems from its antioxidant functions.

Free radicals are highly reactive chemical substances released by many metabolic reactions into cells and tissues. Although there are many necessary biochemical reactions that depend on free radicals, the instability and nonspecific reactivity of these compounds makes them "loose cannons" inside the cell. They are responsible, for example, for the degradation of fats in cells and in foods, where they frequently produce rancid byproducts. Their involvement in the aging process and in the generation of cancer progenitor cells is now widely recognized by the biomedical community. Because of their unbalanced electrical charge due to free electrons, these free radicals attack and break down tissue and many of the essential macromolecules in the cell, including cell membranes and genetic material. This attack contributes to the degeneration of tissue seen in the elderly and to the uncontrolled growth that characterizes cancer.

Vitamin C is a scavenger of free radicals. Ascorbate works directly in the watery environment of the cells to limit the buildup of free radicals, but it also interacts with fat-soluble antioxidants like vitamin E, which act primarily in the lipid-rich areas of the cell. Together, they clean up free radicals in the body before they have a chance to damage or undermine tissue.

This same property of vitamin C also prevents nitrites and nitrates—found abundantly in bacon and other cured meats—from becoming highly carcinogenic and dangerous nitrosamines. To form nitrosamines, nitrites and nitrates must combine with amines, present in the protein of normal diets, in an acidic environment like the stomach. Vitamin C prevents nitrosamine formation by combining with nitrates and nitrites and rendering them harmless.

Nitrosamines are considered one of the primary contributors to gastrointestinal cancers. In a study of the dietary habits of 391 South Louisiana gastric cancer patients, vitamin C consumption was shown to exert a strong protective effect against gastrointestinal tumor formation. The consumption of nitrite-containing smoked foods and cured meats has been associated with an increased risk of cancers among patients examined in this and many other studies.

Some provinces in northern China have extremely high rates of esophageal cancer (EC). The use of alcohol and tobacco, which accounts for 70 percent of the risk for EC in Europe and America, plays a minor role in China. To better understand the cause of this disease, researchers at the Chinese Academy of Medical Science studied the level of nitrosamines excreted in the urine of inhabitants from these high-risk northern areas. They compared these levels to those excreted by inhabitants from a southern, low-risk province and analyzed the effect of vitamin C supplementation on nitrosamine excretion.

Nitrosamine excretion was considerably higher among the high-risk northern Chinese. Investigators found they could bring this level down to that of low-risk southerners by giving northerners moderate doses of vitamin C. Further investigation revealed that northern Chinese consume few fresh vegetables and little fruit, which are the principal food sources of vitamin C. The Chinese investigators concluded that the high level of EC found in northern provinces was directly related to the dietary intake of vitamin C.[32]

These studies demonstrate that daily consumption of vitamin C has a strong protective effect against chemically-induced gastrointestinal cancers. But there is now evidence that vitamin C not only protects against cancer, but may also help cure it.

CONTROVERSIAL CANCER CURE

As a surgeon in a large Scottish hospital, Dr. Ewan Cameron realized cancer research was doing little to ease the suffering or cure the disease of his cancer patients. He began casting about for new ideas to fight this devastating disease. He eventually formulated a method of attack that is outlined in his book *Hyaluronidase and Cancer*.

In this book Cameron focused on hyaluronidase, an enzyme produced by malignant tumors, which attacks the intercellular cement of surrounding tissue. This attack weakens the collagen matrix of surrounding tissue enough to allow a successful cancer invasion. Cameron concluded that any drug that would fight this enzyme and improve the natural defenses of the host might provide real benefit for cancer patients.

For several years, Cameron tried hormone therapy on his most advanced cancer patients. None of his preparations had any noticeable positive effect. Upon learning that vitamin C inhibits hyaluronidase, builds collagen, and strengthens the immune response, Cameron began giving ascorbic acid to his patients. At the same time, Pauling was proposing that vitamin C might be of help in the fight against cancer. The two began corresponding in 1971 and enjoyed a long and fruitful collaboration.

Cameron prescribed 10 grams of vitamin C per day for hundreds of his cancer patients. Unlike his hormone preparations, vitamin C administration demonstrated significant therapeutic benefits. Patients experienced a greater sense of well-being, less pain, and higher survival rates. After five years, Cameron gathered the survival data for 100 patients given vitamin C therapy and compared them to the survival rates of 1,000 matched historical controls. He found that vitamin C increased the survival of his cancer patients fourfold over the controls. In 1978, Cameron and Pauling published the results of this study.

The Pauling-Cameron cancer study led to heated debates within the medical community—debates that are still raging. Their study was criticized on methodological grounds, and few researchers believed a simple nutrient like vitamin C could positively impact as complex a disease as cancer. The highly renowned Mayo Clinic in Rochester, Minnesota, attempted to duplicate Cameron's findings in two controversial studies, both federally funded by the National Institutes of Health.

The first Mayo Clinic trial found that vitamin C had no effect upon the survival rates of terminal cancer patients. Pauling, Cameron and their growing list of supporters severely criticized this trial because its subjects had gone through devastating chemotherapy, which would have suppressed their immune systems to the point where vitamin C could have been of little benefit. Accepting this criticism, the Mayo Clinic group tried again. The second study once again found the vitamin C group had survival rates identical to those of the placebo groups.

According to Pauling and Cameron, the second study was more flawed than the first. For example, the placebo was easily identifiable, and the controls were not monitored to determine whether they were taking vitamin C on their own. Only six of the 50 controls were tested—and these only one time—for urine levels of vitamin C. One of them excreted over 1,200 mg of vitamin C and the others nearly 500 mg.

Although the Mayo Clinic doctors described this level of vitamin C excretion as "negligible," it is in fact extremely high. Unsupplemented cancer patients normally excrete no more than 10 mg of vitamin C per day. This excretion level is strong evidence that control patients were taking vitamin C on their own, and it renders the study invalid because the control group was not the untreated comparison group intended by the investigators. Significantly, a group of patients who refused to take part in the study, presumably because they did not wish to take vitamin C, had only about half the survival rate of either the supplemented or the control group.

To make these methodological matters worse, the Mayo Clinic research team stopped giving vitamin C to its test patients after only two and a half months. Abrupt termination of high-dose vitamin C therapy produces a syndrome called the "rebound effect," which is characterized by a steep decline in blood ascorbate levels and depression of the immune system. It is likely that acceleration of tumor growth accompanied the decline in cellular ascorbate levels. In his clinical practice, Cameron continued his patients on indefinite vitamin C therapy.

At the very least, the Mayo Clinic scientists did not faithfully duplicate Cameron's earlier, successful study. At the worst, they conducted a poorly managed and poorly conceived evaluation of the pharmacologic effectiveness of vitamin C at taxpayer expense. Cameron himself welcomed an independent evaluation of his treatment protocol. In testimony before the U.S. House Sciences and Technology Committee in 1985, he called for an authoritative test of the efficacy of vitamin C cancer therapy, but cautioned that "such a trial must not be carried out by vitamin C enthusiasts nor by bigots, but by fair-minded skeptics, and conducted not in secrecy but in open cooperation using a mutually agreed-upon protocol with particular attention given to ensuring that the controls are not also taking vitamin C."

At this time, clinical successes with vitamin C cancer therapy have not been widely embraced by the medical community, perhaps because of its fear of recommending high dosages of a substance believed to be a simple, "lowly" nutrient.

After evaluating Ester-C and regular vitamin C to assess their ability to prevent the growth of tumor cells in culture, Hugh Riordan, MD and his research team at the Center for the Improvement of Human Functioning in Wichita, Kansas, reported that Ester-C in their tumor model system appears to block processes associated with cancer proliferation.[33] Although this does not prove that Ester-C is tumoricidal, it does suggest that more research work on its potential anti-cancer effect is warranted.

LOWERING CHOLESTEROL LEVELS

How Vitamin C Lowers the Risk of Cardiovascular Disease

In spite of many advances in our understanding of cardiovascular heart disease, CHD remains the leading cause of death among Americans. Over half of all American mortalities—nearly 1.5 million deaths a year—result from CHD or a related disease. One of the most significant risk factors of CHD is elevated cholesterol levels. More specifically, high levels of low density lipoproteins (LDL, or "bad" cholesterol) and triglycerides increase the risk of heart disease; high levels of high density lipoproteins (HDL, or "good" cholesterol) protect against heart disease.

As might be predicted from the enormous number of deaths from CHD, the "typical" adult American has a dangerously high total cholesterol level, a high LDL level, a high triglyceride level and a low HDL level. Americans can, however, do a variety of things to change their dangerous cholesterol counts. They can exercise. They can eat less fat and more fiber (particularly soluble fiber like oat bran and fruit pectins). And they can take more vitamin C.

Cholesterol is an essential sterol. It is manufactured by the body in large quantities and is an essential component of the membranes surrounding every cell in the body. We would die without it yet too much is dangerous. The liver is the primary manufacturing site of cholesterol. It monitors body levels of cholesterol through a complex feedback mechanism in which blood levels, rates of synthesis, and intestinal absorption all come into play. If any one of these factors is out of balance, dangerous levels of cholesterol can result.

Vitamin C is essential for the conversion of cholesterol into bile acids, which are normally excreted. Without optimal levels of vitamin C, cholesterol remains unconverted and accumulates in the body. In a 1973 study, Dr. Emil Ginter, a Czechoslovakian researcher, fed guinea pigs a vitamin C-deficient diet and observed its effects on their blood cholesterol levels. The guinea pigs' production of bile acids decreased, cholesterol accumulated in their livers and blood, and they soon developed hypercholesterolemia, or too much cholesterol in their blood. If kept on the vitamin C-deficient diet indefinitely, the test guinea pigs developed hardened arteries and gallstones.

In humans, vitamin C is effective in lowering the total cholesterol and raising the HDL levels in the blood of subjects with high initial cholesterol, but it has little effect on individuals who already have normal cholesterol levels. In a 1977 trial, Ginter studied 82 persons aged 40 to 80 who consumed a diet containing only 20 mg per day of ascorbic acid. He gave half of these subjects a daily vitamin C supplement of 500 mg, and the other half received a placebo. After three months of supplementation, the cholesterol levels of the vitamin C group had decreased by an average of 13 percent, while the placebo group's average fell by only 4 percent. Subjects with the highest initial cholesterol level experienced the most dramatic decline.[34]

In a follow-up study in 1982, Ginter divided 280 men and women into 14 groups on the basis of their initial cholesterol levels. When supplemented with vitamin C, those with initial cholesterol levels below 200 mg per deciliter (mg/dL) showed little change. But as initial cholesterol levels rose, vitamin C's positive impact became more and more dramatic. The group with the highest average initial cholesterol level, 350 mg/dL, experienced an average decline of 20 percent, or 70 mg/dL, from vitamin C supplementation.[35]

Dr. Anthony Verlangieri and his collaborators at the University of Mississippi have studied the relationship of vitamin C to atherosclerosis, or "hardening of the arteries," in a variety of animal models. It has long been observed that blood vessels of vitamin C-deficient animals are weakened and malformed, and Verlangieri has shown that this effect is even more pronounced when cholesterol is fed. Cholesterol appears to remove important sulfated mucopolysaccharides from the ground substance of the aortic wall and thereby promotes plaque formation. Administration of ascorbic acid reverses this effect and prevents the thickening of the aortic wall that is the hallmark of atherosclerosis.[36]

These and other studies demonstrate that vitamin C supplementation can have dramatic effects on CHD risk factors. Its regular use could save thousands, if not millions, of lives. Evidence from epidemiological studies supports this conclusion.

In 1948, two researchers, L. Breslow and H. D. Chope, interviewed 577 randomly selected residents of San Mateo County, California, who were 50 years old or older. The researchers surveyed physical, mental and environmental factors that might affect their subjects' survivability. Seven years later, they checked back with the subjects to see who had survived—and why. Of all the factors they analyzed, Breslow and Chope found the intake of vitamin C to have the most profound effect on mortality—even more than cigarette smoking.

At any age, a smoker has twice the chance of dying as does a nonsmoker. But, according to Breslow and Chope, someone whose diet is low in vitamin C (averaging 24 mg per day) has 2.5 times more risk of dying in a given period than someone with a diet high in vitamin C (averaging 127 mg per day). For example, a large glass of orange juice daily would easily provide 127 mg of vitamin C per day. Although foods with high levels of vitamin C may contain a variety of other beneficial ingredients, no other nutrient than vitamin C has been shown to have such a significant impact on mortality.[37]

Vitamin C supplementation may be particularly effective in reducing the risk of mortality in the aged. The elderly are at the greatest risk of chronic degenerative diseases like cancer and CHD, and they often have suboptimal body stores of vitamin C. Inadequate nutrition in the elderly is caused by a variety of factors. The elderly are frequently institutionalized, where meals are often poorly planned, poorly prepared or unappetizing. The elderly also show poor absorption and retention of many nutrients, vitamin C and other water-soluble vitamins in particular. With age, proper nutrition therefore becomes more difficult but increasingly important. Vitamin C supplementation can have a highly beneficial effect on the health of the elderly.

VITAMIN C METABOLITES

THE MYSTERY, THE SCIENCE, AND THE MAGIC

The profound biological effects of high doses of vitamin C have led many researchers and health professionals to appreciate that large doses of vitamin C behave differently in the body than smaller, nutritional doses. The body changes vitamin C into numerous metabolites that may have physiological actions different from those of vitamin C itself. And these metabolites—whether manufactured in the body or ingested along with supplemental vitamin C—may influence how the vitamin itself is transported and utilized. The level of these metabolites in the body may not rise significantly, however, until very large doses of vitamin C are administered.

Both the reduced and oxidized forms of ascorbate possess vitamin C activity, because both forms are interchangeable in the body. They are metabolized quite differently in biological systems, however. Compared to the reduced ascorbate, the oxidized form—dehydroascorbate—is relatively unstable and, after being converted to diketogulonate, completely loses its vitamin C activity. As shown in the diagram below, diketogulonate can be broken down into a variety of smaller fragments by many cells. Chief among these metabolites are oxalate and threonate. Some metabolites are excreted, while others appear to remain in the body and perform other functions.

Figure 1. Metabolism of Vitamin C.

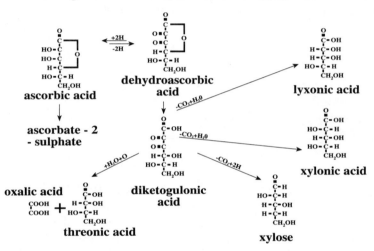

Oxalate excreted in urine has been viewed with some concern because it is a component of one type of kidney stone composed of the highly insoluble calcium oxalate. Numerous studies conducted to test the actual impact of vitamin C supplementation on urinary oxalate excretion have demonstrated that supplementation has little effect on urinary oxalate levels. In one study, Dr. Karl-Heinz Schmidt and his colleagues gave daily doses of 10 grams of ascorbic acid to five healthy male volunteers and measured their subsequent urinary oxalate levels. None experienced a dramatic rise in oxalate levels.[38] Many clinicians currently believe that slight increases in urinary oxalate due to vitamin C supplementation would be a problem only in a small number of individuals—called "stone formers"—who are considered to be prone to this condition.[39]

On the other hand, threonate and other aldonic acids significantly influence vitamin C uptake and utilization. The studies of Anthony Verlangieri, PhD of the University of Mississippi have laid the groundwork for our better understanding of how these metabolites interact with vitamin C in the body. His work has shown that C metabolites—especially threonate—are directly involved with increased blood levels of vitamin C.

Verlangieri and his colleague, Dr. Michael Fay, have used isolated cells in culture to model how vitamin C is utilized by various body tissues. They have used cells from laboratory animals, as well as humans, to study influences on vitamin C utilization. Their studies have used types of cells that are widely regarded as representative of skin cells and of cancerous cells. In a number of careful experiments, they observed that exposing cells to calcium threonate increased the uptake of ascorbic acid by both cell types. Other aldonic acids were shown to have a similar effect.[40]

ARE HIGH DOSES OF VITAMIN C
OR C METABOLITES HARMFUL?

Significant amounts of dehydroascorbate (DHA) may be present in all vitamin C supplements, since DHA can be formed as a result of ascorbic acid's exposure to air, moisture, heat or light. Because ascorbate and DHA simply represent two sides of the same coin, both possess vitamin C activity when taken orally. Almost 50 years ago, when vitamin C research was in its infancy, there were some reports from laboratory animal experiments that DHA could damage pancreatic cells and cause diabetes if injected directly into the bloodstream in large amounts. These early studies created some alarm but were unrealistic from the standpoint of conventional oral usage of vitamin C supplements. Numerous studies have shown that orally ingested DHA has no toxicity; on the contrary, it is equivalent to ascorbate as a source of antiscorbutic vitamin C.

Whether ascorbate or DHA or even one of the other C metabolites represents the biologically active form of vitamin C is an important question that cannot yet be answered. Nearly all the vitamin C in the body is present as ascorbate because cells and tissues maintain themselves in a "reduced" state. Because of this, all but small amounts of dehydroascorbate are reduced back to ascorbate. Even these low concentrations of DHA may exhibit unexpected antioxidant properties. For example, it has been suggested that DHA has a beneficial antioxidant effect even greater than ascorbate's in protecting low-density lipoproteins (LDL) from becoming oxidized and from becoming atherogenic, that is, involved in the process of "hardening of the arteries."[41]

When threonate is fed to animals at doses much higher than those encountered during vitamin C supplementation, no toxicity has been observed. The most interesting effect of feeding threonate by itself—and this offers a clue to its natural function in the body—is to mobilize the ascorbic acid stored in many tissues and to make it available for metabolism.[42]

Vitamin C in its various forms is probably the least toxic substance in the arsenal of supplemental nutrients or pharmacologic agents. The U.S. Food and Drug Administration evaluated all aspects of the metabolism and potential toxicity of ascorbates prior to adding them to its list of "generally recognized as safe" (GRAS) approved substances for food and oral use.

The haphazard use of high-dose vitamin C supplements can result in a condition called the rebound effect. Discussed earlier, the rebound effect is a real danger for those who engage in "yo-yo" supplementation with high levels of vitamin C. If you wish to end a program of intensive supplementation, you should taper off gradually. Do not abruptly halt vitamin C supplementation. Your body is slow to adapt to this dietary change, and it will metabolize essential reserves of vitamin C before adjusting to the reduced intake, leaving you with mild scurvy and probably worse off than when you started supplementation.

The only negative side effect of regular large doses of vitamin C seems to be gastrointestinal discomfort and diarrhea. These effects are due in large part to the acidity of ascorbic acid itself. A new technology has been developed to manufacture a vitamin C that circumvents many of these problems. At the same time, this new process introduces important metabolites of vitamin C so that they are present along with ascorbate when the supplement is taken. The Inter-Cal Corporation of Prescott, Arizona, utilizes a unique manufacturing process that neutralizes the acidity of ascorbic acid and maximizes the formation of dehydroascorbate, threonate, and other aldonic acids so they can work synergistically to speed the absorption and utilization of vitamin C. This technology has received U.S. Patent No. 4,822,816. The ascorbate/C metabolite complex is sold under the trade name Ester-C® ascorbate and is produced in five different mineral forms: calcium, magnesium, zinc, potassium and sodium.

This family of products has been tested in many different situations where high-dose vitamin C supplementation is used. It is now available for use in a variety of nutritional, topical, dental, and veterinary applications. Unlike many ordinary dry-mixed mineral ascorbates, the Ester-C product is tightly bonded with a mineral, making it potentially more absorbable. In addition, the Ester-C product is prepared using only deionized water and pure starting ingredients, unlike other metal ascorbates prepared by the Ruskin process in organic solvents such as alcohol or acetone.[43] The way in which vitamin C is neutralized during manufacturing produces the natural metabolites of vitamin C that are responsible for so many beneficial pharmacologic actions. The C metabolites make up a significant percentage of the Ester-C preparations.

Easier on the Stomach

One of the immediate benefits of neutralized vitamin C is its gentle digestion and assimilation. Ascorbic acid by itself is acidic. When it reaches the alkaline environment of the lower intestinal tract, it can cause inflammation of the intestinal tissue, gas, diarrhea and discomfort. This syndrome usually results from very large doses of vitamin C, and it can limit vitamin C's absorption.

Buffering vitamin C with a mineral to produce a more neutral ascorbate moderates its acidity, but uncomfortable symptoms can still result from large doses of an ascorbate. When an ascorbate reacts with the acid of the stomach, carbon dioxide or "gas" is often the result. Neutralized Ester-C, however, is pH buffered and fully reacted with its mineral.

Ester-C Bioavailability

A number of human and animal studies have explored the absorption and physiological effects of Ester-C® mineral ascorbates in comparison to normal vitamin C. These studies have yielded exciting new information about the nature of vitamin C and its metabolites.

In one animal trial, Dr. Anthony Verlangieri and his colleague, Marilyn Bush, fed two groups of rats equal amounts of either ascorbic acid or Ester-C. They tested the blood and urine levels of vitamin C in these animals for four hours after oral administration. The animals fed the Ester-C had higher blood levels of vitamin C, suggesting an improved rate of absorption in comparison to normal vitamin C. Vitamin C was not detected in the urine of the Ester-C group until long after it was discovered in the urine of the group fed normal vitamin C. This delay in excretion suggests better tissue utilization of the Ester-C before it "spilled over" into the urine. Verlangieri stated that this improved absorption and tissue uptake appeared to be due to the vitamin C metabolite threonic acid, which is present in Ester-C.[44]

Except for some bats and the guinea pig, all lower mammals, including the rat, manufacture their own vitamin C. One strain of rat—the Japanese ODS rat—is defective in its ability to manufacture its own ascorbic acid, however, and ODS rats are now widely used by vitamin C researchers for laboratory studies of this nutrient. These rats develop scurvy if they do not have a source of vitamin C in their diet.

Drs. Verlangieri and Fay took advantage of the inability of ODS rats to manufacture ascorbic acid to evaluate the bioavailability of Ester-C calcium ascorbate.[45] To one group of mildly vitamin C-deficient ODS rats, they administered Ester-C calcium ascorbate containing metabolites. The minimum dose of Ester-C to prevent scurvy was determined after 24 days. When an equivalent amount of ordinary vitamin C was administered, it was inadequate to prevent scurvy. The results of this experiment further confirmed that, in an animal model, Ester-C is more bioavailable than normal vitamin C.

In 1990 this concept was tested in humans by Jonathan Wright, MD of the Kent-Meridian Clinical Laboratory in Washington State.[46] The human bioavailability study was designed to compare the absorption, retention and utilization of Ester-C and ordinary vitamin C. Absorption was measured by vitamin C levels in the plasma fraction of blood. Retention was inferred from the urinary vitamin C levels at different times after supplementation. Finally, tissue utilization was assessed by measuring the amount of vitamin C in white blood cells, which are known to accumulate and utilize large amounts of vitamin C for many physiological functions.

Figure 2. Utilization of Ascorbic Acid and Ester-C Compared.

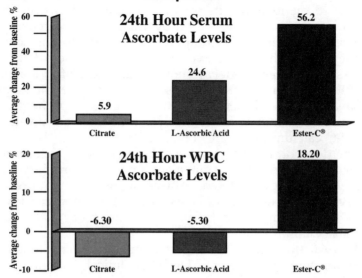

A more focused study of Ester-C's effectiveness was performed recently in San Diego by Dr. Howard Hunt, Professor Emeritus of the University of California San Diego, and Dr. Thomas Rice of the Life Management Group with a group of men enrolled in a corporate fitness program. They wished to see if Ester-C would significantly increase tissue levels of vitamin C in infection-fighting and immunological cells, as measured by uptake of ascorbate into the white blood cells.

Their research plan was very similar to that of Dr. Wright's earlier study. The subjects began with a two-week washout period to stabilize their vitamin C intake at low levels. Groups of 18 men each then received a one-gram oral dose of ascorbic acid in one of three product forms: ascorbic acid, Ester-C calcium ascorbate, and the Ester-C ascorbate with a standardized 3 percent calcium threonate level. White blood cells were isolated from blood samples removed at intervals of 0, 1, 2, 4, and 24 hours from the time of administration.

Hunt and Rice discovered that, with time, the ascorbate

from all supplements steadily accumulated in white cells, but that Ester-C ascorbate and the Ester-C with added threonate reached levels of 300 percent and more than 400 percent, respectively, above the final baseline level attained with ordinary ascorbic acid. They concluded that Ester-C calcium ascorbate/threonate complex provides a superior way to build vitamin C reserves in the important immunocompetent cells of the blood, even using modest levels (one gram) of supplementation. The standardized threonate group showed further intracellular increases of ascorbate; this is the subject of ongoing studies.

At present, the weight of the evidence concerning the bioavailability of Ester-C seems to indicate it is different from that of normal vitamin C, and it appears to benefit from the presence of threonate and other vitamin C metabolites which help improve its absorption and tissue uptake. Dr. Verlangieri's work on the influence of threonate on the absorption of vitamin C and possibly other nutrients clearly shows that this vitamin C metabolite which is present in Ester-C enhances absorption.

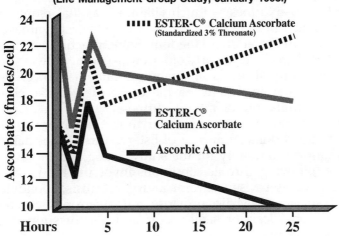

Figure 3. Human White Blood Cells.

(Life Management Group Study, January 1995.)

VETERINARY STUDIES

The improved absorption and retention strongly suggest that the presence of C metabolites confers an amplified physiologic action on Ester-C compared to ordinary vitamin C. This assumption is supported by a growing body of evidence from practitioners who have begun recommending Ester-C in place of normal ascorbate. Many turned to Ester-C calcium ascorbate in the first place because it was a gentle way of administering Vitamin C to dogs and horses without gastrointestinal upset. Because Ester-C was gentler in the stomach of animals, it could be given in the higher doses necessary to achieve certain pharmacologic actions.

Some of the most extraordinary results have been obtained by veterinarians who have searched for innovative and safe ways to treat intractable conditions in dogs and horses. The superior value of Ester-C ascorbate was recently demonstrated in a Norwegian study of arthritic dogs.

Because dogs are among the majority of mammals that manufacture their own ascorbic acid, veterinarians would not ordinarily think of giving them supplemental vitamin C. As can be seen in Table 2, presented earlier, dogs manufacture five to six times as much vitamin C as that required by the human, but they still have one of the lowest synthesizing capacities in the animal kingdom. Some practitioners speculate that dogs—particularly older ones—do not always manufacture optimal levels of vitamin C and that lower tissue levels of vitamin C may be the cause of arthritis, chronic joint inflammation, or muscle stiffness.

Dr. Geir Erik Berge, a veterinarian in Oslo, Norway, gave 100 disabled dogs 30 mg/kg of Ester-C three times daily for six months. To qualify for the study, a dog had to have one of the following chronic conditions involving the joints and connective tissue: severe joint injury, arthrosis, spondylosis, hip dysplasia, older disc prolapse, muscle atrophy as a result of functional loss, or senile wear and tear in support and motion systems.

Dr. Berge measured the success of supplementation in improving the condition of the dogs after one week, six weeks and six months through clinical evaluations using a scoring system, as well as reports from the dog owners. Because of the chronic nature of these joint disorders and their resistance to conventional therapy, Dr. Berge did not include a control group of animals, since their outcomes could have been predicted. Berge's study demonstrated significant results.

After one week of treatment with Ester-C, some 75 percent of the ailing dogs showed dramatic improvement in their conditions. This percentage improvement remained relatively stable for the rest of the study; by the six-month mark, 78 percent of the previously suffering dogs had experienced a significant reduction in symptoms. To Berge, the conclusion was inescapable that dogs manufacture suboptimal concentrations of vitamin C in some tissues under the stress of certain ailments. He recommended therapy with Ester-C ascorbate to help correct those deficits.[47]

Guided by Berge's success with degenerative diseases in dogs, Dr. L. Phillips Brown conducted a similar study with dogs housed at the Best Friends Animal Sanctuary in Kanab, Utah. Dr. Brown administered Ester-C calcium ascorbate, ordinary ascorbic acid, or a placebo twice daily to groups of dogs for three weeks. Response to treatment was graded with the Average Mobility Improvement Score (AMIS), using a four-point scale, with "0" representing no response and "3" representing a very good response. Treatment was then discontinued for three weeks, and the groups were crossed over so that each group received a different treatment. Treatment and scoring were performed two more times in this fashion.

When all improvement scores were added up, Dr. Brown found that dogs receiving the Ester-C ascorbate showed an AMIS score of 1.52, while dogs receiving plain ascorbic acid showed an AMIS score of 0.7. The average score of the placebo was 0.04—indicating that no significant improvement can be expected if no intervention is performed. In addition to showing that Ester-C calcium ascorbate was about three times more effective than ordinary ascorbic acid for these conditions, Dr. Brown's study also pointed out that there is no real cure for degenerative joint conditions in dogs and that improvement can be expected only when supplementation is given.[48,49]

Figure 4. Average Mobility Improvement Scores (AMIS).

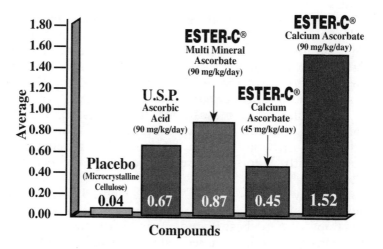

Horses also manufacture endogenous ascorbic acid, yet there is growing evidence that the amount produced may not be sufficient to counter the effects of age, husbandry and athletic demands. Dr. N. Lee Newman realized that vitamin C supplementation might help with the treatment of degenerative joint disease (DJD) of horses she frequently sees in her veterinary practice in Middletown, Virginia. In 1992, she began clinical trials of oral Ester-C calcium ascorbate for horses diagnosed with a variety of DJD conditions exhibiting moderate to severe lameness.

Dr. Newman began to record radiographic evidence and degree of response to treatment, using the American Association of Equine Practitioners Lameness Classification Scores. At the conclusion of the 18-month trial period, over 90 percent of the horses had shown good to excellent response to the Ester-C calcium ascorbate supplement. More significantly, 80 percent of the "improved" horses remained sound and usable even after the supplement was discontinued. These exciting new results demonstrate the importance of alternative modalities and therapeutics for the treatment of many conditions formerly thought to be hopeless.[50]

CHEWABLE VITAMINS: PUBLIC ENEMY #1?

The pathology of dental disease is complex. It is known to be influenced by many factors including nutrition, genetics and the regularity of home and professional oral care. It is by now well documented that the acid produced by bacteria living in close contact with tooth enamel—called plaque—can produce erosion and dental caries. Certain species of oral bacteria can also produce toxins that destroy collagen, leading to erosion of dental filaments and bony tissue, and to eventual loss of teeth—all of which characterize periodontal disease.

The association of vitamin C with oral health has been established since the earliest days of interest in treating scurvy. Early manifestations of scurvy include foul breath due to gum erosion and loss of teeth due to degeneration of connective tissue, bone and enamel. This remarkable association has prompted numerous investigators to ask whether periodontal disease is one manifestation of subclinical scurvy. In any case, adequate amounts of dietary vitamin C are the first line of defense against dental disease.

Many individuals and families with small children utilize the so-called chewable forms of ascorbic acid as a way of ingesting vitamin C and reaping the benefits of vitamin C for oral health. They do not realize that this practice can put their teeth in jeopardy! It is not generally appreciated that even mildly acidic conditions can cause the tooth enamel to dissolve in exactly the same way that plaque bacteria cause tooth decay.[51] Once the outer protective layer of tooth enamel has been stripped away, the underlying sensitive dentin structures become vulnerable to more rapid environmental erosion.

Dr. Steven Silverstein, Dr. Grayson Marshall, and Larry

Watanabe of the University of California Dental School in San Francisco have documented this remarkably rapid process in a series of elegant experiments utilizing scanning electron microscopy. They showed that dilute solutions of plain ascorbic acid (containing amounts that would be typical in the mouth after chewing ascorbic acid supplements) caused definite erosion of intact human tooth enamel within one minute of exposure. After just a few minutes, the degree of enamel loss is shockingly apparent in the micrographs. By comparison, teeth exposed to equivalent concentrations of vitamin C as Ester-C calcium ascorbate remained completely unaffected. The side-by-side comparison of this process is revealed in the following photographs:

Figure 5. Action on Tooth Enamel of Ascorbic Acid and Ester-C Compared.

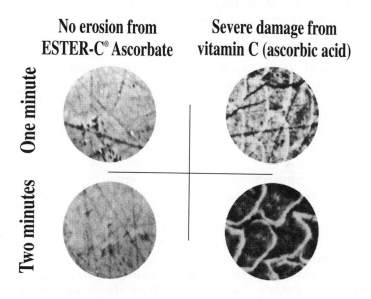

No erosion from ESTER-C® Ascorbate — Severe damage from vitamin C (ascorbic acid)

One minute / Two minutes

Anti-Plaque Activity

Recently, much dental research has focused on ways of reducing tooth decay by preventing the growth of bacteria that colonize the tooth surface. Two species in particular—*Streptococcus mutans* and *Streptococcus sobrinus*—are notorious culprits in plaque formation. It has become increasingly popular to add zinc compounds to mouth rinses and toothpastes for their bacteriostatic properties. It is not well known yet that one of the Ester-C mineral ascorbates can accomplish the same result—and provide necessary vitamin C at the same time.

Dr. Charles Hoover, working with Dr. Silverstein in San Francisco, performed a study of the bacteriostatic effects of an Ester-C zinc ascorbate compared to a commonly used zinc salt. They grew the Streptococcus bacteria mentioned above in separate cultures so they could measure how many of the bacteria were able to attach themselves to a glass surface. Using this technique, they could mimic the way these bacteria create plaque on the surface of tooth enamel. They found that the Ester-C zinc ascorbate was able to provide the same minimal inhibitory activity toward bacterial growth as an equivalent concentration of a zinc compound that has been commonly used in dental health products. In addition, the Ester-C can provide important amounts of vitamin C to strengthen periodontal tissues.

A GENETIC DISEASE

WHAT WE LOST AND WHAT WE GAINED

Irwin Stone was a chemist who had studied vitamin C since 1934. He advanced a theory that humans stopped producing their own vitamin C through an evolutionary accident rather than through biochemical design. This accident left humans with a genetic disease called hypoascorbemia—the final, and fatal, symptom of which is scurvy. In its less acute form, hypoascorbemia prevents humans from dealing with a variety of other common chronic health problems such as hypercholesterolemia, coronary heart disease, colds, cancer and arthritis.

To prove his point, Stone noted that nearly every other mammal has taken an evolutionary path toward greater endogenous production of vitamin C. Stone used the goat as a good example of a mammal that does not suffer from this genetic disease or any of its complications. Goats and humans weigh about the same, but the goat produces between 2.2 and 13.3 grams per day of ascorbic acid. Goats 2: Man zero. Stone's theory explains why vitamin C supplementation has such a profound impact on so many different health problems. If common chronic and acute health problems stem from—or are aggravated by—a genetic mistake that deprived man of adequate levels of ascorbic acid, then it makes perfect sense for everyone to supplement his or her diet with vitamin C to overcome this devastating defect.

CONCLUSIONS

Vitamin C supplementation is proving to have surprisingly beneficial effects on every aspect of human health. It relieves the symptoms of the common cold and flu for many people. It helps fight other viral and bacterial infections. It strengthens the body's defenses and may help fight cancer. Ascorbic acid supplementation improves the cholesterol counts of those with dangerous cholesterol levels and reduces the risk of cardiovascular heart disease. And it is particularly beneficial to the elderly to help them combat the tissue and joint degeneration due to oxidative damage.

Ester-C ascorbates make supplementation even easier and more beneficial. Their pH neutrality makes them gentler on the digestive system than even buffered ascorbic acid. Because they contain high concentrations of threonate and other C metabolites, they are more effective at fulfilling the physiologic potential of vitamin C than other forms. Ester-C ascorbates are better absorbed, better retained, and more effectively utilized by cells and tissues.

The take-home messages are clear—vitamin C and its metabolite-containing companion Ester-C are nutrients which are important beyond the prevention of scurvy. The tremendous explosion of scientific and clinical information on the health benefits of consuming a diet which contains significantly more than the RDA of vitamin C seems to confirm Dr. Pauling's position expressed nearly 30 years ago— that vitamin C may be the most important health-protecting nutrient ever discovered to reduce the risk of today's common age-related diseases. Beyond this is the exciting possibility that metabolite-containing products like Ester-C improve absorption and tissue utilization of vitamin C in areas of specific clinical need. We are witnessing the emergence of a new field of nutrition which goes beyond preventing deficiency to understanding how nutrients like vitamin C can promote optimal health.

REFERENCES

1. Block G. Vitamin C and cancer prevention: the epidemiologic evidence. *American Journal of Clinical Nutrition* 1991; 53(suppl):270S-82S.
2. Scaccini C, Chiesig G, Jialal I. A critical assessment of the effects of amino guanidine and ascorbate on the oxidative modification of LDL. *Journal of Lipid Research* 1994; 35:1085-92.
3. Anderson R. The immunostimulatory, anti-inflammatory and anti-allergic properties of ascorbate. In: Draper HH, ed. *Advances in Nutritional Research* 1984; New York, NY: Plenum Press; 6:19-45.
4. Abel B. Randomized trial of clomiphene citrate treatment and vitamin C for male infertility. *British Journal of Urology* 1982; 54:780-84.
5. Pauling L. Ascorbic acid and the common cold. *Medical Tribune* 1976; 24:1.

6. Johnston CS, Martin LJ, Cai X. Antihistamine effect of supplemental ascorbic acid and neutrophil chemotaxis. *Journal of the American College of Nutrition* 1992; 11:172-76.
7. Enstrom JE, Kanim LE, Klein MA. Vitamin C intake and mortality among a sample of the United States population. *Epidemiology* 1992; 3:194-202.
8. Read MH, Lauritzen GC. Supplement recommendations by a sample of registered dietitians. *Topics in Clinical Nutrition* 1994; 9:67-72.
9. Subar A, Block G. Use of vitamin and mineral supplements. *American Journal of Epidemiology* 1990; 132:1091-1101.
10. Levine M., Cantilena C. In situ kinetics and ascorbic acid requirements. *World Review of Nutrition and Dietetics* 1993; 72:114-27.
11. Block G. Antioxidant intake in the United States. *Toxicology and Industrial Health* 1993; 9:295-301.
12. Belfield WO, Stone I. Megascorbic prophylaxis and megascorbic therapy. *Journal of the International Academy of Preventive Medicine* 1975; 2:11-16.
13. Klenner F. *Clinical Guide to the Use of Vitamin C.* 1988; Life Sciences Press, Tacoma, Washington.
14. Cheraskin E. The prevalence of hypovitaminosis C. *Journal of the American Medical Association* 1984; 254:2894.
15. Rath M, Pauling L. Solution to the puzzle of human cardiovascular disease. *Journal of Orthomolecular Medicine* 1991;6:125-34.
16. Levine M. New concepts in the biology and biochemistry of ascorbic acid. *New England Journal of Medicine* 1986; 314:892-901.
17. Fay MJ, Verlangieri AJ. Stimulatory action of calcium threonate on ascorbic acid uptake by a human T-lymphoma cell line. *Life Sciences* 1991; 49:1377-81.
18. Frei B, England L, Ames BN. Ascorbate is an outstanding antioxidant in human blood plasma. *Proceedings of the National Academy of Sciences USA* 1989; 86:6377-81.
19. Pauling L. Orthomolecular Psychiatry, *Science* 1968; 160:265-75.
20. Lee W, Davis K, Rettmer R, Labbe R. Ascorbic acid status: biochemical and clinical considerations. *American Journal of Clinical Nutrition* 1988; 48:286-90.
21. Levine M, Cantilena C. See reference 10.
22. *Recommended Dietary Allowances,* 10th Edition. Food and Nutrition Board, National Research Council, National Academy of Sciences. Washington, D.C.: National Academy Press, 1989.
23. Recommended daily allowances for vitamin C. *Proceedings of the National Academy of Sciences* 70:969-972.
24. Eaton SB, Konner M. Paleolithic nutrition. *New England Journal of Medicine* 1985; 312(5):283.
25. Pauling L. *Vitamin C and the Common Cold.* W. H. Freeman, San Francisco; 1970.
26. Terezhalmy GT et al. The use of water-soluble bioflavonoid-ascorbic acid complex in the treatment of recurrent herpes labialis. *Oral Surgery, Oral Medicine, Oral Pathology* 1978; 45:56-62.

27. Anderson RA. *Wellness Medicine.* 1990; Keats Publishing, New Canaan, Conn.: 262.
28. Correa P, Foutham E, Ruiz B. Gastric juice, ascorbic acid after intravenous injection: effect of H. pylori infection. *Journal of the National Cancer Institute,* 1995; 87:52-53.
29. Greene M, Wilson CWM. Effect of aspirin on ascorbic acid metabolism during colds. *British Journal of Clinical Pharmacology* 2:369.
30. Thomas WR, Holt RG. Vitamin C and immunity: an assessment of the evidence. *Clinical Experimental Immunology* 1978; 32:370-379.
31. Harakeh S, Jariwalla R, Pauling L. Suppression of human immunodeficiency virus replication by ascorbate in chronically and acutely infected cells. *Proceedings of the National Academy of Sciences* 1990; 87:7245-49.
32. Shih-Hsin L et al. Urinary excretion of N-nitrosamino acids and nitrate by inhabitants of high- and low-risk areas for esophageal cancer in northern China: endogenous formation of nitrosoproline and its inhibition by vitamin C. *Cancer Research* 1986; 46:1485-1491.
33. Riordan HD. Improved microplate fluorometer counting of viable tumor and normal cells. *Anticancer Research* 1994; 14:927-32.
34. Ginter E et al. Effects of ascorbic acid on plasma cholesterol in humans in a long-term experiment. *International Journal of Vitamin Nutrition Research* 47:123-134.
35. Ginter E. Vitamin C in the control of hypercholesteremia in man. *New Clinical Applications in Immunology, Lipid Metabolism, and Cancer* 1982; p.137-152.
36. Verlangieri AJ, Hollis TM, Mumma RO. Effects of ascorbic acid and its 2-sulfate on rabbit aortic intimal thickening. *Blood Vessels* 1977; 14:157.
37. Chope HD and Breslow L. Nutritional studies of the aging. *American Journal of Public Health* 1955; 46:61-67.
38. Schmidt K-H et al. Urinary oxalate excretion after large intakes of ascorbic acid in man. *The American Journal of Clinical Nutrition* 1981; 34:305-311.
39. Chalmers AH, Cowley DM, Brown JM. A possible etiological role for ascorbate in calculi formation. *Clinical Chemistry* 1986; 32:333-336.
40. Fay MJ, Bush MJ, Verlangieri AJ. Effect of aldonic acids on the uptake of ascorbic acid by 3T3 mouse fibroblasts and human T lymphoma cells. *General Pharmacology* 1994; 25:1465-1469.
41. Retsky KL, Freeman MW, Frei B. Ascorbic acid oxidation product(s) protect human low density lipoprotein against atherogenic modification. Anti- rather than prooxidant activity of vitamin C in the presence of transition metal ions. *Journal of Biological Chemistry* 1993; 268:1304-1309.
42. Thomas M and Hughes RE. Evaluation of threonic acid toxicity in small animals. *Food Chemistry* 1985; 17:79-83.
43. Ruskin SL. U. S. Patent No. 2,400,171. Stabilized metal ascorbates. 1935.
44. Bush MJ, Verlangieri AJ. An acute study of the relative gastro-intesti-

nal absorption of a novel form of calcium ascorbate. *Research Communications in Chemical Pathology and Pharmacology* 1987; 57:137-140.

45. Verlangieri AJ, Fay MJ, Bannon AW. Comparison of the anti-scorbutic activity of L-ascorbic acid and Ester C in the non-ascorbate synthesizing Osteogenic Disorder Shionogi (ODS) rat. *Life Sciences* 1991; 48:2275-2281.

46. Wright JV, Suen RM. Comparative studies of "Ester C" versus L-ascorbic acid. *International Clinical Nutrition Review* 1990; 10:267-271.

47. Berge GE. Polyascorbate (C-Flex), an interesting alternative by problems in the support and movement apparatus in dogs. *The Norwegian Veterinary Journal* 1990; 102:581.

48. Brown LP. Vitamin C (ascorbic acid)—new forms and new uses in dogs. *Proceedings of the 1994 American Holistic Veterinary Medical Association Annual Conference,* Orlando, FL. 1994; pp. 119-125.

49. Brown LP. Vitamin C. New forms and new uses in dogs. *New Editions Health World* Nov/Dec 1994; 44-45.

50. Newman NL. Equine degenerative joint disease. A nutritional approach with Ester-C. *Natural Pet* 1995; in press.

51. Hays GL, Bullock Q, Lazzari EP, Puente ES. Salivary pH while dissolving vitamin C-containing tablets. *American Journal of Dentistry* 1992; 5:269-271.